A LOOK AT US HISTORY



# THE LOUISIANA PURCHASE

BY SETH LYNCH

Gareth Stevens PUBLISHING

CRASHCOURSE

**Please visit our website, www.garethstevens.com. For a free color catalog of all our high-quality books, call toll free 1-800-542-2595 or fax 1-877-542-2596.**

**Library of Congress Cataloging-in-Publication Data**

Names: Lynch, Seth, author.
Title: The Louisiana Purchase / Seth Lynch.
Description: New York : Gareth Stevens Publishing, 2019. | Series: A look at US history | Includes index.
Identifiers: LCCN 2017050824| ISBN 9781538221310 (library bound) | ISBN 9781538221334 (pbk.) | ISBN 9781538221341 (6 pack)
Subjects: LCSH: Louisiana Purchase--Juvenile literature. | United States--Territorial expansion--History--19th century--Juvenile literature. | United States--History--1801-1809--Juvenile literature.
Classification: LCC E333 .L96 2019 | DDC 973.4/6--dc23 LC record available at https://lccn.loc.gov/2017050824

Published in 2019 by
**Gareth Stevens Publishing**
111 East 14th Street, Suite 349
New York, NY 10003



Designer: Samantha DeMartin
Editor: Kristen Nelson

Photo credits: Series art Christophe BOISSON/Shutterstock.com; (feather quill) Galushko Sergey/Shutterstock.com; (parchment) mollicart-design/Shutterstock.com; cover, p. 1 GraphicaArtis/Archive Photos/Getty Images; p. 5 Bardocz Peter/Shutterstock.com; p. 7 Kean Collection/Archive Photos/Getty Images; p. 9 Everett - Art/Shutterstock.com; p. 11 Interim Archives/Archive Photos/Getty Images; p. 13 The New York Historical Society/ Archive Photos/Getty Images; pp. 15, 23, 25 Everett Historical/Shutterstock.com; pp. 17, 21 MPI/Archive Photos/Getty Images; p. 19 UniversalImagesGroup/Universal Images Group/Getty Images; p. 27 Glenn Asakawa/The Denver Post/Getty Images; p. 29 Sipley/Archive Photos/ Getty Images.



Printed in the United States of America

CPSIA compliance information: Batch #CS18GS: For further information contact Gareth Stevens, New York, New York at 1-800-542-2595.

# CONTENTS



Words in the glossary appear in **bold** type the first time they are used in the text.

# ALL ABOUT LOUISIANA

During the mid-1700s, Great Britain, Spain, and France all had large land claims in North America. France had control of a big part right in the middle of the **continent** called Louisiana. It included an important **port** called New Orleans.

## MAKE THE GRADE

Louisiana's borders were from the Mississippi River in the east to the Rocky Mountains in the west, and from Canada in the north to the Gulf of Mexico in the south.

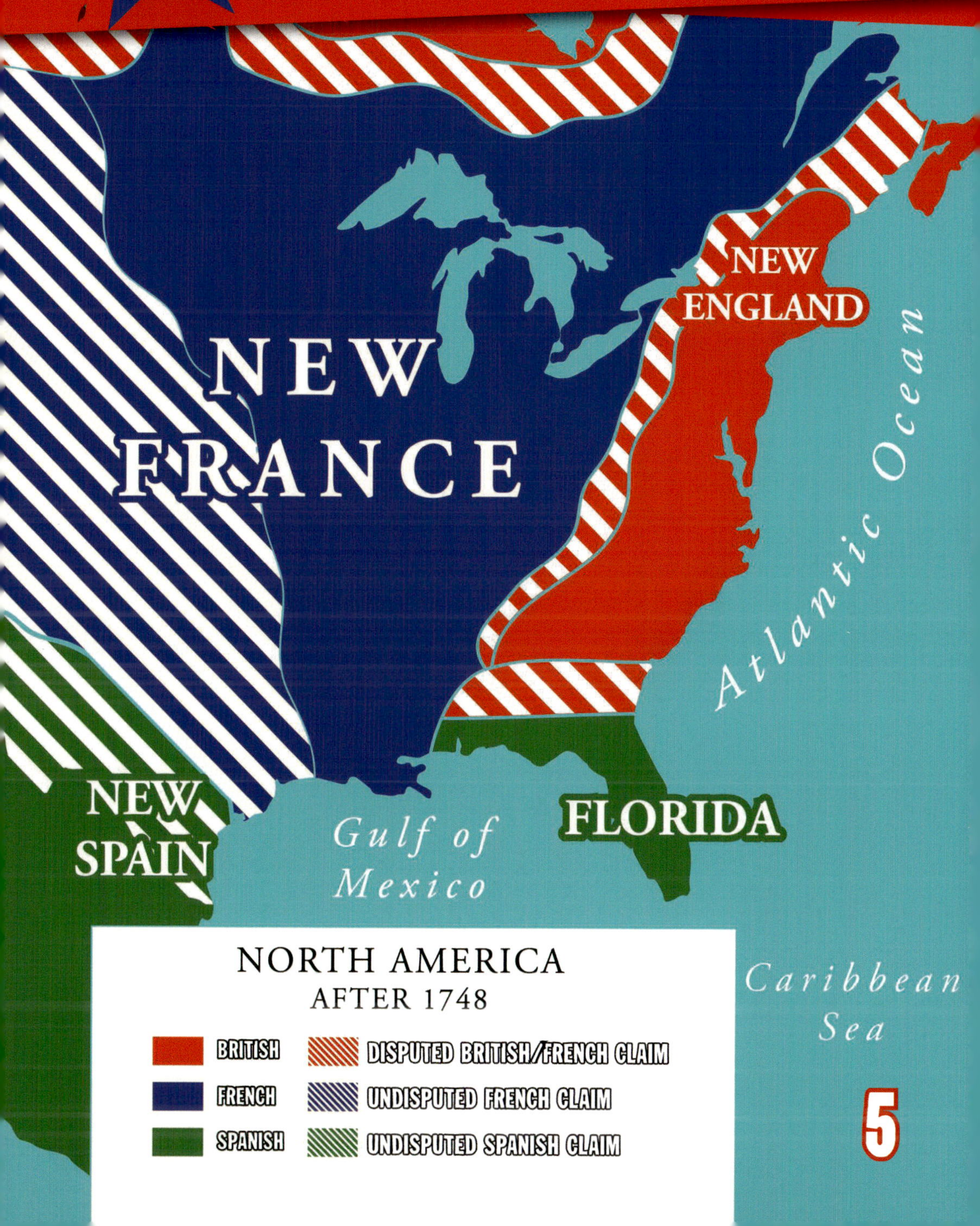

# LAND CHANGES HANDS

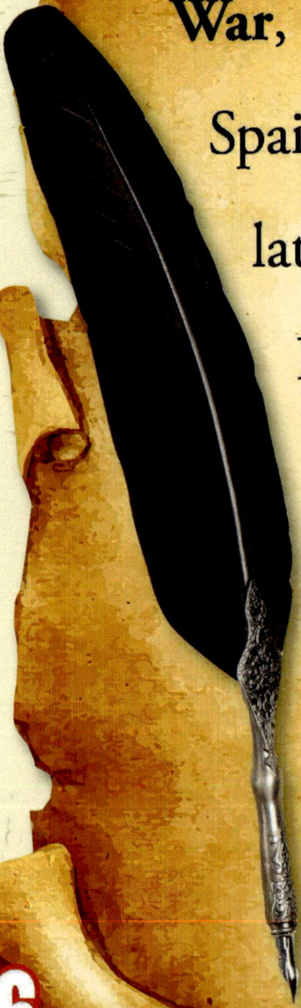

Near the end of the **Seven Years' War**, France **ceded** Louisiana to Spain in 1762. A few months later, in 1763, the **Treaty** of Paris ended the war. This treaty turned over other French land in North America to Great Britain.

## MAKE THE GRADE

Spain also gained control of the Mississippi River and New Orleans. In 1795, the United States made an agreement with Spain so western farmers could use the river and port to ship American-made goods.

# FRANCE RISES

In 1792, the French **Revolution** ended with the French people overthrowing their king. A leader named Napoleon Bonaparte soon rose to power in the new government in 1799. France began regaining power on the world stage.

## MAKE THE GRADE

At first, Napoleon was part of a government called the Consulate. In 1804, he declared himself France's emperor.

# LOUISIANA, FRENCH AGAIN

Napoleon **convinced** the Spanish king to cede Louisiana back to France in the Treaty of San Ildefonso. The treaty took effect in 1802. The US government began to worry that farmers would lose use of the Mississippi and Port New Orleans.

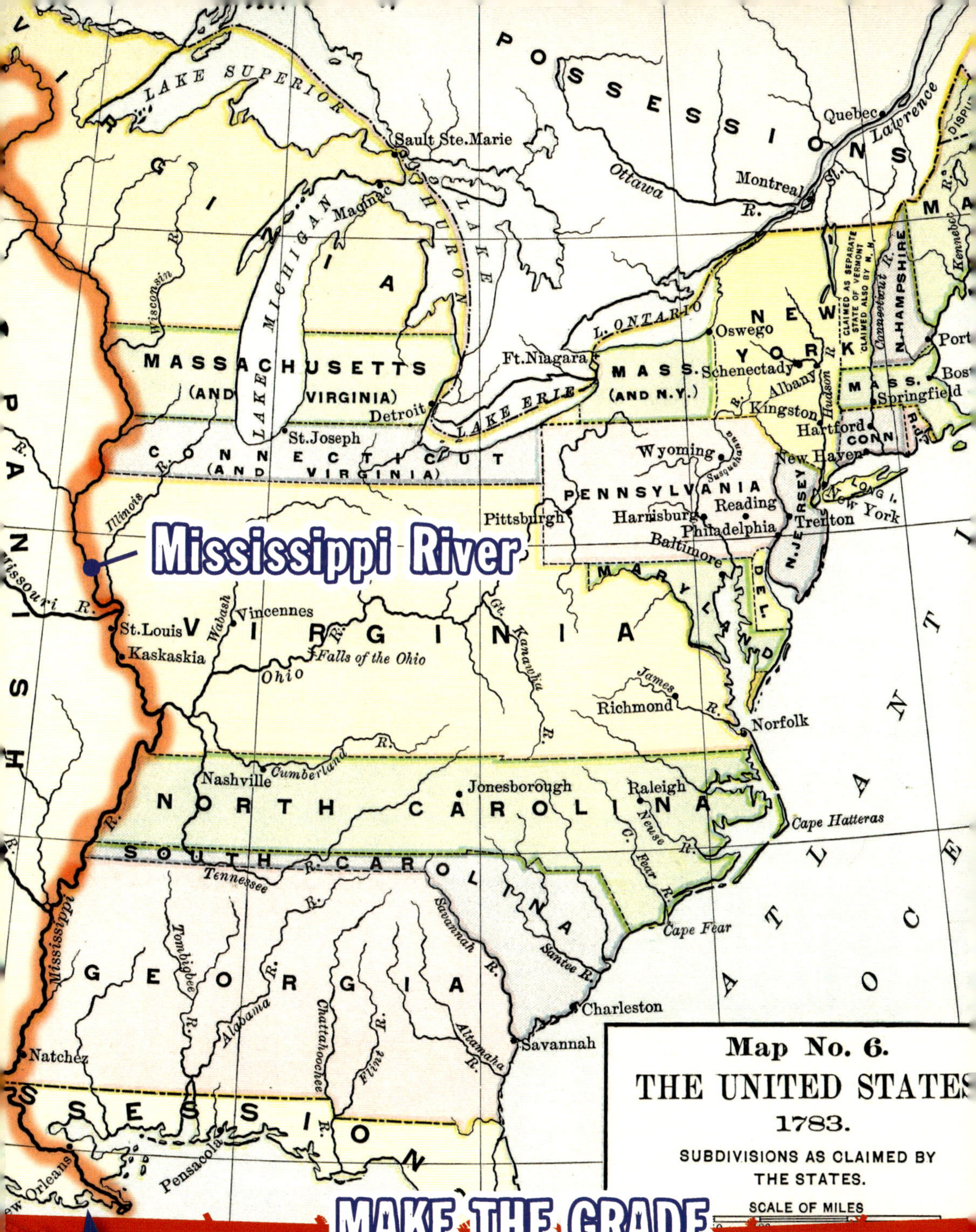


## MAKE THE GRADE

The Mississippi River was the western border of the United States following the American Revolution, the war in which the United States gained independence from Great Britain.

President Thomas Jefferson told the US **minister** in Paris, France, to try stopping France from taking the land back from Spain. If he couldn't, the minister was to offer to buy New Orleans. James Monroe was also sent to Paris to help make a deal.

Robert R. Livingston

## MAKE THE GRADE

The US minister, Robert R. Livingston, told people in France the United States was going to make an agreement with Great Britain. He knew Napoleon wouldn't want that to happen.

# MAKING A BIG DEAL

President Jefferson had said the ministers could only spend up to $10 million on a land deal with France. Livingston and Monroe also weren't given the power to buy all of Louisiana. As they **negotiated** with France, however, a $15 million deal was struck.

## MAKE THE GRADE

Mail from Europe took weeks or months to reach the United States. Livingston and Monroe agreed to the land deal without Jefferson knowing because they didn't want to miss out on it.

President Thomas Jefferson

The treaty selling the Louisiana Territory to the United States was signed on May 2, 1803. When Jefferson got word in July, he was happy about the purchase. He worried whether the Senate, which had to approve the treaty, would agree.

## MAKE THE GRADE

France sold the whole of Louisiana because the country didn't have enough forces to **defend** it. Napoleon also needed money to fight should a war with Great Britain start.

# CONSTITUTIONAL?

Jefferson was unsure the US Constitution gave the president the power to add such a large piece of land to the country. However, the Senate allowed the treaty to stand. About 828,000 square miles (2,144,510 sq km) of land were added to the United States!

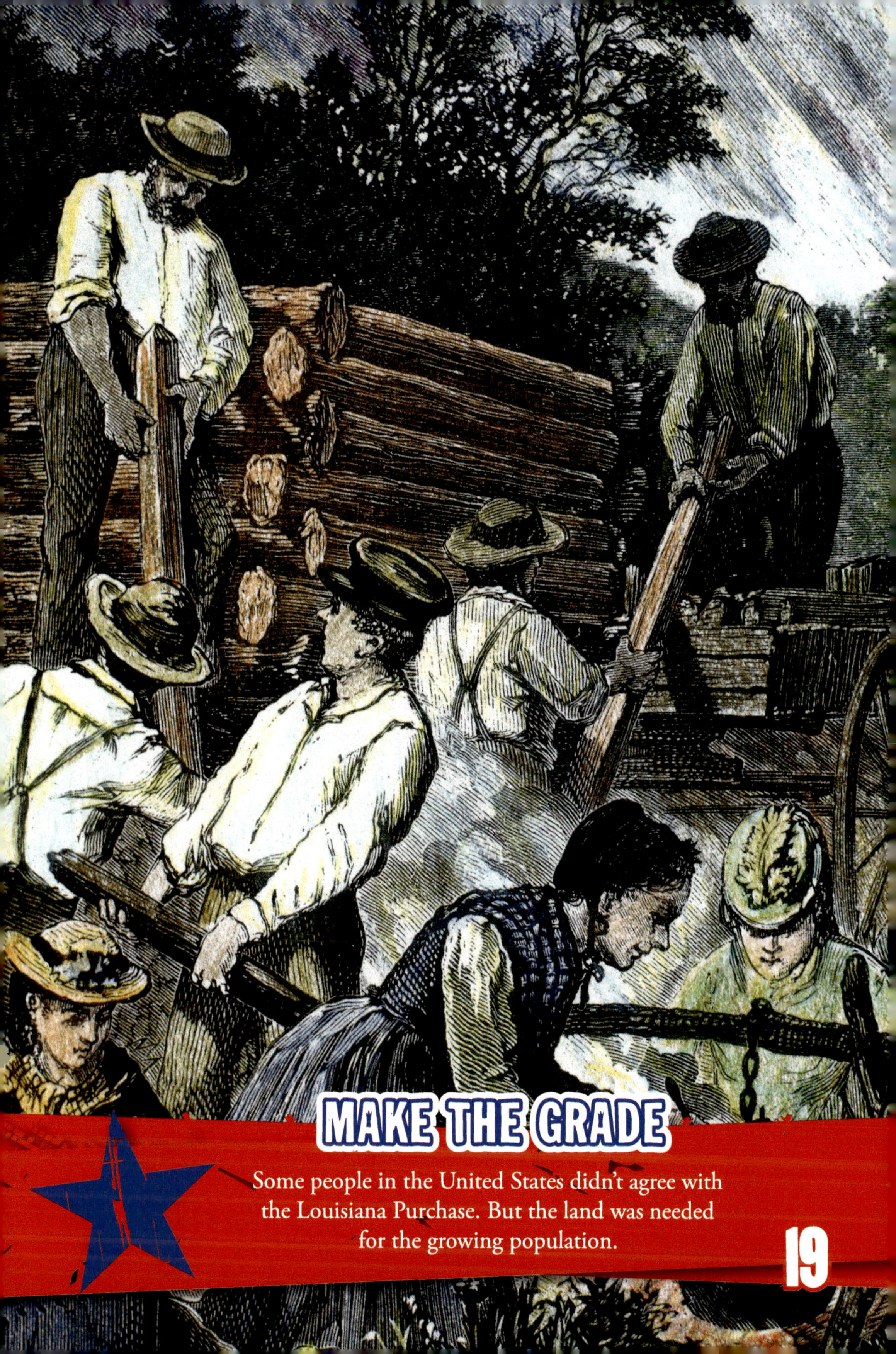

## MAKE THE GRADE

Some people in the United States didn't agree with the Louisiana Purchase. But the land was needed for the growing population.

# LOUISIANA'S BORDERS

Some of the **boundaries** of the Louisiana Purchase weren't clear. The Mississippi was the eastern boundary, and the Rocky Mountains were the western boundary. It took more than 10 years for the United States, Great Britain, and Spain to work out the others.

## MAKE THE GRADE

In 1818, Great Britain and the United States decided on a northern border. In 1819, Spain agreed to boundaries in the southwest as well as modern-day Texas and Florida.

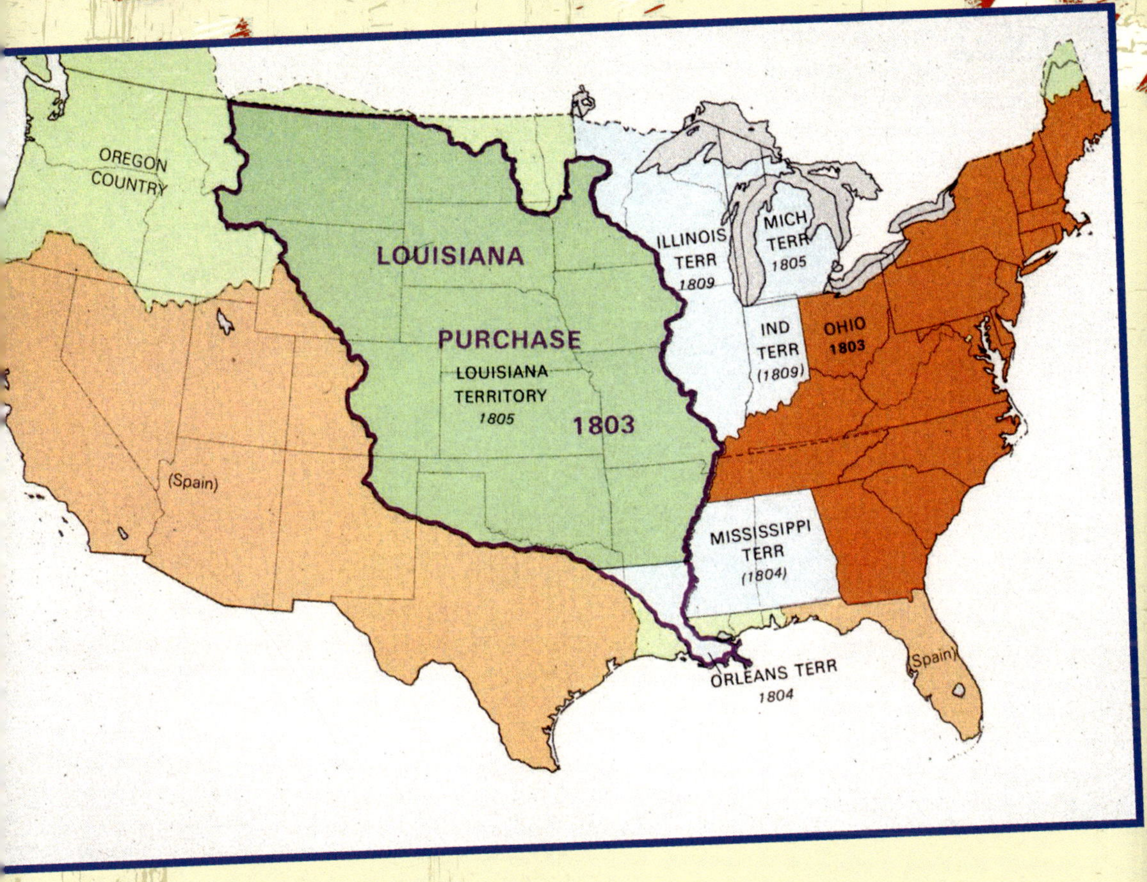

# LEWIS AND CLARK

President Jefferson asked Captain Meriwether Lewis to explore the new Louisiana Territory. Lewis was joined by William Clark and 30 other men. Together, they were called the Corps of Discovery. On May 14, 1804, they set off on the Missouri River.

Meriwether Lewis

## MAKE THE GRADE

Jefferson hoped Lewis and Clark would find a water route to the Pacific Ocean. They thought the Missouri River might be that route.

On their journey, the Corps of Discovery met as many as 50 Native American groups. They added two **interpreters** to their company to help talk with the tribes. One was a French Canadian fur trader. The other was his wife, Sacagawea.

## MAKE THE GRADE

Sacagawea was Shoshone. She had connections to some of the tribes they met along the way. Her baby son traveled with the corps, too.

The Corps of Discovery reached the Pacific Ocean in 1805. They had mapped the new US land as they traveled and gained knowledge of the plants, animals, and native groups living there. Their work would help settlers for years to come.

## MAKE THE GRADE

Lewis and Clark didn't find an all-water route to the Pacific. But, they traveled and mapped many rivers, including the Missouri and Columbia.

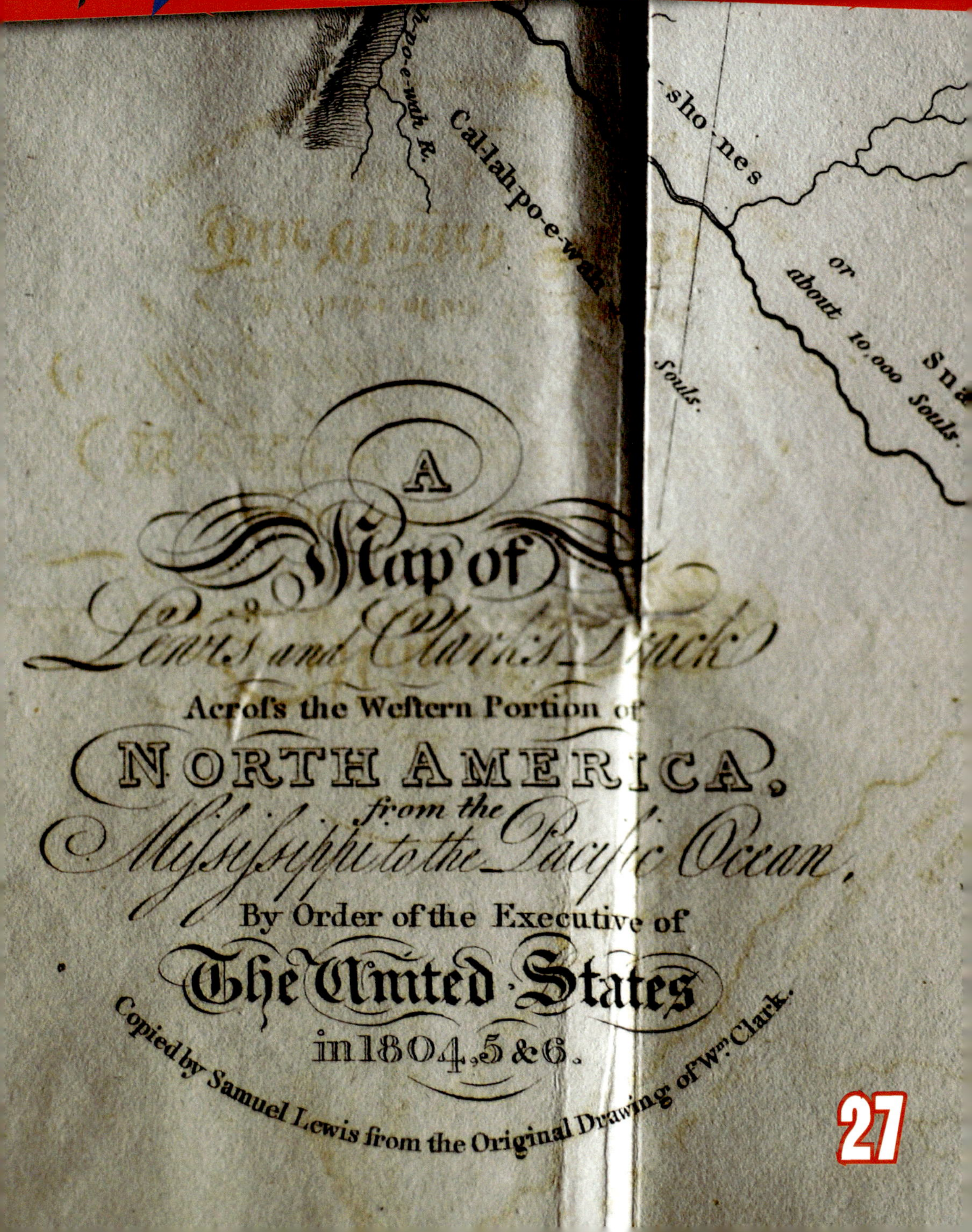

# NEW STATES

The Louisiana Purchase doubled the size of the United States. Soon, it was divided into the states of Arkansas, Louisiana, Missouri, Nebraska, Iowa, Oklahoma, North Dakota, and South Dakota as well as parts of Kansas, Minnesota, Wyoming, Montana, and Colorado.

## MAKE THE GRADE

As new states were added to the United States, issues of whether slavery should be allowed in them created problems in the young nation.

# TIMELINE OF THE LOUISIANA PURCHASE

**November 3, 1762**
France cedes the Louisiana Territory to Spain.

**1795**
Spain grants the United States the right to use the Mississippi River to ship goods made in America through New Orleans.

**1800**
Frances reacquires the Louisiana Territory from Spain and takes it over in 1802.

**January 1803**
James Monroe is sent to France to help negotiate land purchases from France.

**May 2, 1803**
The United States and France sign the Louisiana Purchase Treaty.

**October 1803**
The Senate approves the treaty to buy the Louisiana Territory.

**May 14, 1804**
The Corps of Discovery set off on the Missouri River.

# GLOSSARY

**boundary:** something that marks the limit of an area or place

**cede:** to give control of something to someone else

**continent:** one of Earth's seven great landmasses

**convince:** to make a person believe something

**defend:** to guard against harm

**interpreter:** someone who can tell the meaning of another language

**minister:** a person who goes to a foreign land on behalf of their country

**negotiate:** to come to an agreement

**port:** a city or town where ships can load and unload goods

**revolution:** a movement to overthrow an established government

**Seven Years' War:** a war that lasted from 1756 to 1763 that many powerful countries in Europe took part in. This war included struggles between Great Britain and France about control of North America.

**treaty:** an agreement between countries

# FOR MORE INFORMATION

## Books

O'Donoghue, Sean. *Thomas Jefferson and the Louisiana Purchase*. New York, NY: PowerKids Press, 2017.

Rice, Katelyn. *The Great Leap Westward*. Huntington Beach, CA: Teacher Created Materials, 2017.

## Website

**Louisiana Purchase**

*www.monticello.org/site/jefferson/louisiana-purchase*

Read more about the Louisiana Purchase and find links to other information about President Thomas Jefferson.

**Publisher's note to educators and parents:** Our editors have carefully reviewed this website to ensure that it is suitable for students. Many websites change frequently, however, and we cannot guarantee that a site's future contents will continue to meet our high standards of quality and educational value. Be advised that students should be closely supervised whenever they access the internet.

# INDEX